Treasures

A book of poetry

Nathaliya Silva

BookLeaf Publishing

India | USA | UK

Copyright © Nathaliya Silva
All Rights Reserved.

This book has been self-published with all reasonable efforts taken to make the material error-free by the author. No part of this book shall be used, reproduced in any manner whatsoever without written permission from the author, except in the case of brief quotations embodied in critical articles and reviews.

The Author of this book is solely responsible and liable for its content including but not limited to the views, representations, descriptions, statements, information, opinions, and references ["Content"]. The Content of this book shall not constitute or be construed or deemed to reflect the opinion or expression of the Publisher or Editor. Neither the Publisher nor Editor endorse or approve the Content of this book or guarantee the reliability, accuracy, or completeness of the Content published herein and do not make any representations or warranties of any kind, express or implied, including but not limited to the implied warranties of merchantability, fitness for a particular purpose.

The Publisher and Editor shall not be liable whatsoever...

Made with ❤ on the BookLeaf Publishing Platform

www.bookleafpub.in

www.bookleafpub.com

Dedication

To my dearest mother,
Your love, wisdom, and unwavering support have been the greatest treasures of my life. This book is a testament to the strength and inspiration you have given me every day.

With all my love,

Nathaliya Silva

Preface

Life is a treasure to be treasured.

Welcome to Treasures! This collection is more than just poetry; it embodies the emotions that colour our modern lives.

Treasures is not only my first book but also a true reflection of every dawn and dusk of my life. It captures the joy and peace of mind that inspired me to write these poems.

As you immerse yourself in each piece, you'll uncover a tapestry of themes woven from personal aspirations, nature, and everyday encounters. Each poem offers a glimpse into the hidden treasures within our daily lives.

I extend my heartfelt thanks to all who supported me throughout this creative journey. Your encouragement and feedback have been invaluable.

I hope you find joy not only in reading but also in indulging in the emotions etched in every word.

Happy Reading!

Acknowledgements

The creation of Treasures has been a wonderful journey made possible by the love and support of the incredible people in my life.
To my beloved mother, your unwavering belief in me has been my guiding light. Your love is the greatest treasure I hold, and this collection is a reflection of that bond.
To my family and friends, thank you for your constant encouragement, understanding, and patience throughout this process. Your words of support have carried me through every poem, and your presence has been invaluable.
Finally, to everyone who contributed behind the scenes in bringing this book to life, your dedication and hard work have made this dream a reality.
With heartfelt appreciation,

Nathaliya Silva

When Venus meets the Moon

Above the lavish greenery land, we stood,
Smiling back at the winking trees, we knew,
They must be loving our sight, so we should
Sprinkle more and more love, so we threw.

The flowers giggled with glittery rosy cheeks,
The wind rushed to call the others to see,
The nightingales sang to their highest peaks,
Waiting for us to create a beautiful scene.

So, we did. We kissed, and it made the night remarkable,
No one judged us the way we thought they would be,
Sparkling eyes roamed around to see us as a couple,
On that night, happiness was all we could see.

The Metallic Dragonfly

The metallic dragonfly watches me,
Across the field with its flashy eyes,
A dream I've held since that day,
When I saw my father take off on it.

Now it's my turn to gaze at the dragonfly,
Knowing it's time to board and enjoy a smooth ride,
Ready to carry me away too,
On its back, filled with joy and life.

Once, clouds bade me adieu from above,
Hoping my dreams would come true someday,
As my childhood waited, counting the days,
For this moment to finally arrive.

Now I bid the angelic clouds farewell,
Thanking them for dreams come true,
As I look down on them from above,
Smiling and praying for even better days to come.

Winter Hushes

The gravel- grey shade invades the sky early now,
The gentle cold stiffs the trees and flowers around,
The brutal hush embraces the land in stillness,
It's just the beginning of this so- called charming winter.

Evening skies are no more pleasant to be photographed,
A morning splash of water is what everyone dreads,
A flood of warmth is what everyone hopes aloud,
As winter gives no mercy easily to anyone around.

"A boiling cup of water is what makes us keep going",
Yet does it really keep us going is the doubt I have.
No tea or coffee ever kept me awake in this monstrous
winter,
The charming winter should never be taken for granted.

The Weeping Clouds

Oh my sunshine,
Oh my beloved sunshine.
Who hath cursed you in abundance,
That made you bolt away?

They chased the mightiest source of light,
The energy that kept their lives ever bright.
The most beloved of mine,
Who is no more to be seen in divine.

Now the skies are grey and dull,
With weeping clouds around.
I shall bring forth endless sorrow,
With tears of mine that know no bound.

Kill Zone

Thousand-armed gather in rows,
Filling the mustard brown ground with sores
Guns, swords and other weapons brought along
Making the heavenly earth look so wrong.

Only few seconds it took indeed,
To flood the sacred soil with spilled blood
Regret blood, love blood, parental blood,
All vanished and banished in the name of war.

What more can an innocent armed give,
besides giving up his own precious life for them?
Give up on his love to parents, children and beloved,
In exchange for a filthy foul flood of blood

Do you think your loved fellows can live without thee?
Then how could they?
How inhuman of you to sacrifice immature souls,
To a never-ending nasty flood of revenge.

The revenge ends and you all celebrate in victory,
Whilst others celebrate sorrow in misery.
You all celebrate it with fresh bread and fine wine,
Whilst others celebrate it with fresh tears and fine
whines.

Gazing into the Abyss

Under the dazzling bar light,
In the middle of the strong liquor smell,
Next to the earth-booming music,
I stood, gazing into the abyss.

Our eyes were locked,
Feeling his rough skin on mine,
His eyes burnt with the fear of love,
His gun pointed at my back.

"Wake up, my love, please,"
I whispered into his poor ears,
Which had heard way too much,
"I love you no matter what."

His burning eyes watered with fear,
His lips locked together, teeth gritting,
His swollen cheeks begged for salvation,
His heart skipped beats as he stared at me.

"The sun shines as bright as your love,
The trees cheer for our innocent love,
The roads are deserted, paving us a runaway,
Why don't we elope from this moment?"

He grinned innocently, imagining the dramatic escape,
Slowly pulling the gun toward the dead earth,
Still crying like a desperate, widowed mother,
Touching my soft cheeks with his left palm, kissing me.

"Enough, my love. Enough."
Silence invaded the crazy bar, with its roaring,
unpleasant noise.
I stood there weakly, gazing into the abyss,
Smiling at my own sins—and my love.

Men don't cry

Men don't cry,
They gasp.
Men don't cry,
They inhale.

Why have your eyes been nailed?
'Men don't cry!', they smirk.
Why have your lips been stitched?
'Men don't cry!', they repeat ceaselessly.

Can the word 'manly' ever heal them?
Why can't they unstitch their lips?
Why can't they show their emotions?
Why do men only inhale but not exhale?

They do breathe too.
They do have emotions too.
When sad, they feel like their heart is being stabbed too.
But, 'men don't cry!' comes to their mind too.

Do they have to hide their melancholy for a few words?
Do they have to always pretend to be the strong one?
Do they have to be the hero all the time?
Don't heroes have emotions?

The Naked Princess

Shame on her,
Damn her,
Screw her,
But, what for?

Her lips are sealed,
Her eyes are shut,
Her soul is ripped,
Yet, what for?

For rising to save her kind,
For saying no for matrimony,
For losing her virginity too soon,
or for losing her virginity too late ?

For many other petty reasons,
Her life has already been decided.
She is a marionette of his,
She is a marionette of society.

The Floating Dream

I once had a dream of wearing handful of gold,
Gaudy necklaces covering my neck,
Wiggling my ears to show off my 24 karat gold,
And to swing my hair side to side in prosperity.

Yet, I woke up to the smell of disaster,
Locked up in one place with no way of income,
Eating the cheapest rotis with no rice to be seen,
Living in the dark to save us from the charges.

They did let us go out one day,
The day I hesitated to breathe properly,
Knowing I'll have to sell my remaining pair of bangles,
To feed the mouths of hungry fellows.

What have they done our dreams?
We are counting down days till the end,
Knowing only 2 more bangles are remaining for any,
Not knowing what to do after selling them.

Let Me Go

For I love the moon,
You drew the dark curtains.
For I love the sun, you
Doused its brightness.
For I love the sea,
You hailed a deadly storm.
For I love the flowers, you
Burnt down the whole pitiful garden.
For I love you,
You, you locked me in a damned doom.

Till Death Do Us Apart

Brunette, short, messy hair,
Small, round coffee-brown eyes,
Bags hanging all over her eyes,
Withered and unbothered lips,
With shades of 20s wrinkles.

Pitch-black bra and clashing boxers,
A denim jacket on top, yet nonchalant.
Sneakers running around, dragging her,
Aimlessly to roads she has never traveled,
Holding hands with him. Only him in her aloof world.

They stared at each other, knowing it was just them,
Against the 'real' world. They walked past the quiet
lakes,
The serene train stations, the peaceful parks,
Calm, dazzling city lights. It was just them. Just them.
Knocking on people, she still followed her sneakers. And
him.

She received a beautiful, heartwarming kiss along with a
red rose.
Her face lifted to his; "You might need them," he said.
She smiled and closed her eyes softly to feel his breath
and his never-dying
Smell of existence. Tears escaped her small eyes, gliding
on their way.
His fingers lingered into her pitiful body, pulling her
close to his warmth.

"Love me one more time," she whispered with a huge
smile on her face.
A huge smile of utter distress, frustration, fear, and
agony. She opened her eyes and
Left the rose in front of his last resting place. She looked
up to feel his presence, yet
Felt nothing but his smell of love. The smell of love that
promised to live with her.
"Till death do us apart," she whispered for the last time
and walked away. Alone

My Dear Monster

Dear monster,
My dear Monster,
What are you doing over yonder?
You aren't supposed to be a jester!

With those raging eyes you rush to me,
For I am the beautiful prey of thee,
Waiting for you to tear me into pieces,
Waiting till my love for you increases.

Yet, what have they done to my dear monster?
Once a monster, now a jester!
How could they do this to thee?
Please, rush to me once again with those rageous eyes
and damn me.

The trampy prey did you wrong, didn't she?
She made a lamb out of my wolf,
A drastic change made by her to thee,
Made the monster in you a witless calf.

My dear monster, you were blinded by the wittiness of
hers!
My dear monster, you were too busy being the lovely
monster to her!
My dear monster, the trampy prey made the monster in
you a blur!
My dear monster, the witless calf she buried in you lost
me!

The Curse of Love

One, two, three,
How many times should it be given a pity chance?
How many times should love be forsaken?
How many times should love pretend to be at ease?

One was the time love was blinded by it.
It deceived love by bringing the moons and the stars,
The mountains and the rivers,
The whole universe and back.

Two was the time love was recovering from her bland
sight.
Love began to see the dark side of the moon and the
stars,
The falling of mountains and the shallowness of the
rivers,
The emptiness of the universe and no back.

Three was the time love realized that she had been
deceived by her own blindness.
Now, love realized that she was taken for granted,
She was trampled, disgusted, and played.
She was deceived.

Love cries in pain.
Love smiles in revenge.
Love grins in cruelty.
Pain, revenge and cruelty which was planted by it.

Let Me In

"It's been 8 long years,
It's time to give me a chance, Janice."
"No, he's long gone to the world but not to me."
"It's not fair for me, I love you, can't you see? "
"I don't care, Ben. He'll always be with me."
"It's fine, but let me have a chance."
"No, I don't want to give even a single glance."
"Let me give you the world,
Let me give you what you deserve!"
"What do I deserve, Ben?"
"Everything, Janice. From love to care to strength to a
proper life back again."
"I don't want to enter into your cocoon with him in my
mind."
"It's fine!"
"Stop saying it's fine!"
"Let him be in your mind but I want you to be in my
divine.
Cry, mourn and weep, but in my arms, aligned.
Let me console you through your sleepless nights,

Let me hold your hands during your weakest times,
Just let me in, Janice."
"Oh Ben, you poor one. You will never fathom my
sorrows, my weaknesses and my worst."
"Then let me know. Make me understand. Give me all
your sorrows, Janice."
"How can I do this to you?"
"You can, my dear. Trust yourself. Trust me. I won't let
him down, Janice. I promise, I will carry both your love
and mine."

So Tender

You glided into my chat,
And made me believe that
Love is so amusing and delicate.
Your glide was so tender for me to,
Not have time to run away.

You skimmed into my eyes,
And made me believe that
Love is so fair and gentle.
Your skim was so tender for me to
Not have time to gather my thoughts.

You slid into my heart,
And made me believe that
Love is so beautiful and honest.
Your slide was so tender for me to
Not have the thought of running away.

You sailed into my life,
And made me believe that
Love is so eerie and bizarre.
Your sail was so tender for me to
Not have the heart to forget you.

You've sailed so fast into my life,
That I no longer know what is mine.
You made me believe that love is
So tender and so magical and,
Drifted apart like mist.

So tender was your coming,
Yet, so bitter was your drifting.
So tender were your lies,
Like the sparkle in your eyes,
Which shattered me into countless pieces.

The Hostage

The dark room seemed like paradise,
The lack of food seemed delightful,
The smell of fear seemed fascinating,
The sight of torture seemed pleasing.

What was I even thinking?
When he wrenched my hair generously,
Staring into my eyes with his sharp gaze.
I fell in love!

What was he even thinking?
When I smiled through the pain of torture,
Staring into his eyes with my swollen gaze.
He fell in love?

One Day

I shall, one day, walk under the beaming moon,
Feeling truly content with all that surrounds,
Not feeling bothered about your deep voice,
Calling my name and whispering, "I'm sorry"

Till then, I shall walk under this saddening moon,
Wishing I was feeling the warmth next to you,
Not feeling numb for a moment any soon,
Yet only feeling the warmth of my dear blues.

I shall, one day, walk under the humming birds,
Feeling utterly satisfied with my life instincts,
Not feeling bothered about your dreamy glance,
Satisfying me in the most unique ways of all.

Till then, I shall walk under the mourning doves,
Wishing I was resting my heavy head on your chest,
Feeling the bittersweet ache of your memory,
When you only whispered, "Wish you were here"

That Smile

From the little, sparky smirks to,
Breathless, heart-touching eye contact,
We stood there, unsure of what it meant.
Yet, that smile was the definition of divine
And I got lost in the divinity on purpose.

Let us catch each other's sight for the very,
Last time before we could ever drift apart.
One last look from those glittery eyes, and
One last smile from that heavenly purgatory,
Will do the magic for the rest of my life.

Let's Run Away

Is true love real?
Will our true love live?
The moonlight seems perfect,
For us to escape this reality.

Pack your necessities, and let's run away from this
cruelty.
It won't be hard because I'm your only necessity,
And we well deserve this intensity.
So, are you ready for this?

Look! The moon is beaming so beautifully, paving us the
best path,
The stars are blushing, seeing our love.
Isn't this fate?
Isn't this great?

Let's escape this cruel reality,
Where love is being measured,
Where love is being labeled,
Where true love is hard to exist.

Look! The trees are waving us adieus,
The mountains are closing their eyes for us to French
kiss,
The rivers are giving us the most heavenly music.
So, what are we waiting for?

Let's escape this sad reality,
Where true love is being mocked,
Where written text comes before true love,
Where God's words of loving another are being ignored.

Look! The owls are mating with true love in their eyes,
The wonderful breeze is showering us with the essence
of dance.
Let's dance the night away,
Let's dance the real away.

Let's escape this weird reality,
Where love exists only until one's thirst is quenched,
Where love exists only for one night,
Where love exists only for one's might.

Look! We are almost there,
We are almost in our paradise.
Our true love will be written everywhere:
The streets, the books, the papers, and where not.

Let's escape this non-existing reality,
Where love like ours is being hindered,
Where our love cannot be shown,
Where our love is hard to live.

Look! We are here.
We made it together.
The greatness of our love is living.
The greatness of our fate is shining.

The Forbidden Love

You say when the sunlight comes out,
We can part ways like we never knew each other.
But it's dawn already, and we are still here together,
Breathing into each other, making love.

I want to hold you, kiss you, and lose myself in you,
Pull you into my arms and let you know for the very last
time
How much you mean to me, yet
You choose to walk away once the light comes out.

I want to dance with you, comfort you, and make a home
with you,
Push you out of that little box of yours and show you
where the horizon is.
But you choose to walk away in shame,
Down the cracked and dirty road of yours once the sun
comes up.

The sun comes out, and you walk away,
Your face looks swollen and soft already.
The sight of you leaving makes me weak.
Oh, only if I could pull you out of that hell.

Give Me One More Chance

Give me one more chance to figure it out,
Give me one more chance to make it all right.
Act smart? How smart?
Act cunning? That sounds funny!

Baby girl, the world is too cunning for you,
The world is too tough for that silly soul.
Baby girl, chin up and act right,
Before you lose to the big ones.

Give me one more chance to think, all right?
Give me one more chance to turn it upside down.
I didn't know the world could be this fearful,
I didn't know the world could be this hateful.

Baby girl, stomp on the steps they stomp on,
Drink the water they drink from.
Baby girl, be vicious for what they do,
'Cause you might have to do the same to pace up.

Give me one more chance to be the vicious woman,
Give me one more chance to pace up with them,
For this is pretty new for me,
Yet, give me one more chance.

www.ingramcontent.com/pod-product-compliance
Lightning Source LLC
La Vergne TN
LVHW041248200726
843507LV00013B/2858